Santa Monica Public Library

I SMP 00 2753130 S

DISCARD

D0788356

FAIRVIEW BRANCH
Santa Monica Public Library

MAR - - 2018

Start to Finish
Second Series

FROM Egg TO Owl

JENNIFER BOOTHROYD

LERNER PUBLICATIONS Minneapolis

Copyright © 2017 by Lerner Publishing Group, Inc.

All rights reserved. International copyright secured. No part of this book may be reproduced, stored in a retrieval system, or transmitted in any form or by any means— electronic, mechanical, photocopying, recording, or otherwise—without the prior written permission of Lerner Publishing Group, Inc., except for the inclusion of brief quotations in an acknowledged review.

Lerner Publications Company
A division of Lerner Publishing Group, Inc.
241 First Avenue North
Minneapolis, MN 55401 USA

For reading levels and more information, look up this title at www.lernerbooks.com.

Library of Congress Cataloging-in-Publication Data

Names: Boothroyd, Jennifer, 1972– author.
Title: From egg to owl / by Jennifer Boothroyd.
Other titles: Start to finish (Minneapolis, Minn.). Second series.
Description: Minneapolis : Lerner Publications, [2016] | Series: Start to finish, second series | Audience: Ages 5–9. | Audience: K to grade 3. | Includes bibliographical references and index.
Identifiers: LCCN 2015048774 (print) | LCCN 2015050989 (ebook) | ISBN 9781512418316 (lb : alk. paper) | ISBN 9781512418378 (pb : alk. paper) | ISBN 9781512418385 (eb pdf)
Subjects: LCSH: Owls—Development—Juvenile literature. | Owls—Juvenile literature.
Classification: LCC QL696.S8 B584 2016 (print) | LCC QL696.S8 (ebook) | DDC 598.9/7—dc23

LC record available at http://lccn.loc.gov/2015048774

Manufactured in the United States of America
1-41175-23183-3/4/2016

TABLE OF Contents

Owls are amazing birds. How do they grow?

First, an owl finds a nest.

Owls don't usually build their nests. They use old nests built by other birds. Many have nests in trees, but some have nests on or under the ground. Some owls add feathers or leaves to make the nest warm and soft.

She lays her eggs.

The female owl lays her eggs in the nest. Some owls can lay up to thirteen eggs, but more often, they lay three or four. Owl eggs can be many different shapes and sizes. **Owlets** grow inside the eggs.

Next, she incubates her eggs.

The skin of the female owl's **brood patch** warms the eggs and helps the owlets grow. The male owl brings the mother food so she doesn't have to leave the nest.

Soon the owlets hatch.

The owlets start to hatch in about a month. They use a hard point on their **beak** called an **egg tooth** to break out of their egg. Owlets have only very thin feathers when they hatch, so their mother keeps them warm.

The owlets learn to eat.

The parents bring food to the owlets. Owls eat **prey** such as rabbits, mice, insects, and small birds. First, the parents give them small pieces, but later, the owlets can eat mice and bugs in one gulp.

The owlets explore outside their nest.

The owlets are growing bigger. They are beginning to explore their **habitat** by climbing out of the nest and watching from nearby branches or ledges. They flap their wings to stretch their muscles.

Soon the owlets grow bigger feathers.

An owlet's feathers start out soft and fluffy. Then stronger feathers begin to grow. These special feathers help owls fly silently. The owlets start to look more like their parents.

Then the owlets learn to fly.

The owlets have grown their thicker feathers, so it's time for them to try flying. The owlets don't fly very far because flying takes a lot of energy. They need to grow stronger.

Finally, the owls can live on their own!

After many weeks of practice, the owls have become very good fliers. Their parents don't need to bring them food. The young owls **hunt** for their own food. Soon they will find a **mate** and will be ready to lay their own eggs.

Glossary

beak: the hard mouthpart of a bird

brood patch: an area of skin with few feathers that birds use to keep their eggs and chicks warm

egg tooth: a hard bump on the beak of a bird used to break out of its shell

habitat: the natural home of an animal

hatch: to break out of an eggshell

hunt: to chase an animal to eat

incubates: sits on eggs so they will stay warm and hatch

mate: the male or female partner of a pair of animals who produce young together

owlets: baby or young owls

prey: animals that are hunted for food by another animal

Further Information

Cornell Lab of Ornithology—All about Birds: Great Horned Owl Cam
http://cams.allaboutbirds.org/channel/46/Great_Horned_Owls
Visit this site to view a great horned owl nest up close. If the birds aren't
nesting yet, scroll down to find video of the past year's highlights.

Hirsch, Rebecca E. *Snowy Owls: Stealthy Hunting Birds*. Minneapolis:
Lerner Publications, 2016. How do owls catch such small and quick prey?
Read this book to find out.

Idaho Public Television—Owls: Facts
http://idahoptv.org/dialogue4kids/season12/owls/facts.cfm
Uncover more facts about the lives of owls.

Marsh, Laura. *Owls*. Washington, DC: National Geographic, 2014.
Discover the many different owl species in this book.

O'Shaughnessy, Ruth. *Owls after Dark*. New York: Enslow, 2016. Read
this book to discover how owls live in the darkness of night.

Index

Photo Acknowledgments
The images in this book are used with the permission of:
© David Hosking/Minden Pictures, p. 1; © iStockphoto.
com/Kaphoto, p. 3; © Dfikar/Dreamstime.com, p. 5;
© Vasiliy Vishnevskiy/Dreamstime.com, p. 7; © Michael S.
Quinton/National Geographic/Getty Images, p. 9;
© Wayne Lynch/All Canada Photos/Alamy, p. 11;
© Zorn, Leonard/Animals Animals, p. 13; © iStockphoto.
com/IPGGutenbergUKLtd, p. 15; © Amit_Parashar/iStock/
Thinkstock, p. 17; © Christian Heinrich/imageBROKER/
Alamy, p. 19; © iStockphoto.com/sduben, p. 21.

Front cover: © Michael Callan/FLPA/Corbis.

Main body text set in Arta Std Book 20/26.
Typeface provided by International Typeface Corp.

LERNER
e
SOURCE

Expand learning beyond the printed book. Download free, complementary educational resources for this book from our website, www.lernersource.com.